the gift
of healing

Ron Phillips

**CHARISMA
HOUSE**

Most CHARISMA HOUSE BOOK GROUP products are available at special quantity discounts for bulk purchase for sales promotions, premiums, fund-raising, and educational needs. For details, write Charisma House Book Group, 600 Rinehart Road, Lake Mary, Florida 32746, or telephone (407) 333-0600.

AN ESSENTIAL GUIDE TO THE GIFT OF HEALING by Ron Phillips
Published by Charisma House
Charisma Media/Charisma House Book Group
600 Rinehart Road
Lake Mary, Florida 32746
www.charismahouse.com

Unless otherwise noted, all Scripture quotations are from the New King James Version of the Bible. Copyright © 1979, 1980, 1982 by Thomas Nelson, Inc., publishers. Used by permission.

Scripture quotations marked NAS are from the New American Standard Bible. Copyright © 1960, 1962, 1963, 1968, 1971, 1972, 1973, 1975, 1977 by the Lockman Foundation. Used by permission. (www.Lockman.org)

Scripture quotations marked NIV are from the Holy Bible, New International Version. Copyright © 1973, 1978, 1984, International Bible Society. Used by permission.

Scripture quotations marked NLT are from the Holy Bible, New Living Translation, copyright © 1996, 2004, 2007. Used by permission of Tyndale House Publishers, Inc., Wheaton, IL 60189. All rights reserved.

Cover design by Justin Evans
Design Director: Bill Johnson

Visit the author's website at www.ronphillips.org.

Library of Congress Cataloging-in-Publication Data:
Phillips, Ron M.
   An essential guide to the gift of healing / Ron Phillips.
      p. cm.
   ISBN 978-1-61638-492-0 (trade paper) -- ISBN 978-1-61638-630-6 (e-book)   1. Spiritual healing. 2. Jesus Christ. I. Title.
   BT732.5.P48 2012
   234'.131--dc23
                                          2011044558

While the author has made every effort to provide accurate telephone numbers and Internet addresses at the time of publication, neither the publisher nor the author assumes any responsibility for errors or for changes that occur after publication.

First Edition

12 13 14 15 16 — 987654321
Printed in the United States of America

CONTENTS

Section Three: Healing Through Today's Church

SECTION ONE

An Introduction to Supernatural Healing

CHAPTER ONE

Healing and the Abundant Life

OUR LORD JESUS Christ came that believers might live what He called an "abundant life."

> The thief does not come except to steal, and to kill, and to destroy. I have come that they may have life, and that they may have it more abundantly.
>
> —JOHN 10:10

The word *abundant* translates from a word in the original Greek that means "a life with no lack which goes beyond the ordinary."

The same verse indicates that it is the stated goal of Satan to kill, steal, and destroy. Those three words paint a picture of the cause of sickness and disease in our world. The word *steal* comes from the Greek word *klepsee*, from which we get our word *kleptomaniac*. Satan's obsession is to steal all that we need in our lives, especially our health.

The word *kill* is not the usual word for kill. It is the word *thusee*, which means "to blow on a fire or to blow the smoke of a sacrifice." It came to mean "to slaughter" or "immolate for the purposes of sacrifice." Its implication is that Satan will cause diseases to spread like fire so that your life might be a sacrifice to Satan's evil intent.

The third word is *destroy*, translated from the word *apolesee*, which means "to break down and destroy." This is what sickness does to the human body. It is interesting that all three of these verbs are in the "aorist tense," which means "once and for all." Satan's unyielding desire is to break down people's health, destroy their purpose, and finally kill them.

Jesus came and died that we might live a life that is abundant, that goes beyond what is ordinary. In 3 John 2, the great apostle John writes:

> Beloved, I pray that you may prosper in all things and be in health, just as your soul prospers.

Here John blesses his readers by conveying God's gracious intent for all believers.

The word *health* comes from the word *hugiaino*, from which our English word *hygiene* is derived. It means "to be healthy, well, whole, uncorrupted by disease." This little verse will form the basis for this entire study. There are several keys to understanding healing in Scripture that are hidden in this verse.

First, the word translated *pray* is the word *euchomai*, which means "to wish one well." This implies prayer, but it indicates that those for whom this prayer is released have some choice in the matter. Our prayers and wishes for others to be healed also requires right choices by those for whom we are praying.

Second, the word *prosper* comes from two Greek words, *eu* and *hodos*, which together mean "good journey." It came to mean success from right choices on the journey. This includes material prosperity and physical health. Again, healing requires right belief and right lifestyle choices.

This indicates that there are already healing instincts in the body that work when we make right choices. These choices can include faith, prayer, and also medical treatment. If I get a severe cut, I can choose to have a doctor stitch it, but my body must heal the wound.

Several years ago, the retina in my right eye detached, and I went blind in my right eye. When this happened, I prayed for healing; I also went *immediately* to a retina specialist who reattached it! After the retina is reattached, a gas bubble holds it in place for ninety days. I asked my doctor the day after surgery if it worked. He said, "Ask your boss," speaking of God! He had put it together, but only God could complete the healing.

Also, John adds "as your soul prospers." The word *soul* comes from the Greek word *psuche*. This word is also often translated as "mind." This helps us to understand that our health and healing flow from right thinking *and* right choices. It is important to pray but also important to choose to live healthy.

The goal of this book is to build faith so that you can

appreciate God's gift of healing purchased by the blood of Christ, whatever form that healing might take.

A second goal is to celebrate the preciousness of life that is given to us by God. There is a mystery surrounding those who are challenged in body by injury or disease, that in spite of everything we do they remain in that condition. Yet these are some of the most faithful and productive Christians.

For all that we understand about physical healing, we know it is temporary. We live in a body that is the last remnant of Adam's fall. Paul called our bodies "…the body of this death" (Rom. 7:24, NAS). All earthly healing is temporary, and ultimate healing will happen for us all at the resurrection.

I'm reminded of a scene from the classic film *The Robe*. Marcellus, the chief centurion present at the crucifixion of Jesus (who won the titular robe in the casting of the lots, and who, incidentally has been tormented with nightmares and guilt ever since), is tracking down Christians to create a list of followers when he encounters a crippled woman named Miriam. This beautiful woman is the picture of peace, joy, and hope. Marcellus ridicules her by pointing out that though she claims Christ could work miracles, He left her as He found her. She explains to Marcellus that Jesus could have healed her body, and then "it would have been natural for me to laugh and sing; and then I came to understand that He had done something even better for me…. He left me as I am so that all others like me might know that their misfortune needn't deprive them of happiness within His kingdom."[1]

The joyful truth, however, is that physical healing is possible in this life. With that in mind, it is my desire to explore every possible way to activate healing in our lives. This book will examine every avenue that leads to healing and health. As I send this study forth, I do so humbly as one still seeking to know the mind and will of our Lord Jesus Christ.

> There is healing at the fountain,
> Come and find it, weary soul,
> There your sins may all be covered;
> Jesus waits to make you whole.
> There is healing at the fountain,
> Look to Jesus now and live,
> At the cross lay down thy burden;
> All thy wanderings He'll forgive.
>
> There is healing at the fountain,
> Precious fountain filled with blood;
> Come, oh come, the Savior calls you,
> Come and plunge beneath its flood.
>
> Oh the fountain!
> Blessed healing fountain!
> I am glad 'tis flowing free;
> Oh the fountain!
> Precious, cleansing fountain!
> Praise the Lord, it cleanseth me.[2]

CHAPTER TWO
Healing and the Mystery of Illness

ANY DISCUSSION OF healing must begin with the fundamental question, "What is the origin of sickness?" When it comes to healing, we must also address the question of suffering, the cause of injury through accidents, and sickness and injury due to crime, inhumanity, and war. From a biblical perspective, it is clear that all evil and its consequences are a result of the fall of man in Adam.

Man (male and female) came from God's hand and His breath for God's glory. Read what was revealed in Isaiah 43:7:

> Everyone who is called by My name, whom I have created for My glory; I have formed him, yes, I have made him.

This idea is given some elaboration by the apostle Paul in Ephesians 1:11–12:

> In Him also we have obtained an inheritance, being predestined according to the purpose of Him who works all things according to the

counsel of His will, that we who first trusted in Christ should be to the praise of His glory.

The Westminster Shorter Catechism is a list of questions used to teach children in the faith and lead them to maturity in Christ. The very first question in this catechism is: "What is the chief end of man?"[1] The answer is a glorious truth: "To glorify God and enjoy Him forever!" Man's purpose in life is to know God through Christ and take joy in that relationship. In Mark 12:30, Jesus taught that the greatest commandment is that we love God with all our capacity:

> And you shall love the LORD your God with all your heart, with all your soul, with all your mind, and with all your strength. This is the first commandment.

Mankind was created in the image of God. In that image man differs from the animals. Humanity was endowed with a mind to think, a heart to love, and a will to choose. God allowed man's will to be tested by the tree of the knowledge of good and evil. It was man's wrong choice that plunged our race into the misery of sickness, injury, and death.

When Adam sinned, he began to die. He died *immediately* in his spirit. He was disconnected from fellowship with God. Do not be confused; this is the worst death. He died progressively in his soul (mind, thinking). We see the evidence of this in children. Yes, the terrible twos are, well, terrible, but children are rarely capable of the kind of evil found demonstrated by adults. And Adam died ultimately, as do we all, in his body.

Salvation reverses that curse! When one receives Christ, his spirit comes to life, his mind can be renewed, and ultimately his body will be raised from the dead. That new body will be sinless, sick-less, and deathless!

Among the last remnants of Adam on earth is the human body. This body ages and is subject to illness, injury, and even death. This body carries earth's cursed limitations; Romans 8:29 says that we are being "conformed to the image of His Son." Because God's image is breaking through, humanity can start the process of being like Jesus and health can come to us!

Sickness and the Wrath of God

Sickness, injury, and death are, therefore, the work of Satan released to all humanity and to the earth by Adam's wrong choice and its timeless consequences. It is clear that sickness in Scripture is viewed as a judgment of God. However, knowing that, let me quickly clarify that sickness, like rain, falls on the just and the unjust. Sickness is a temporal judgment brought to the earth by Satan through humanity's wrong choices.

Today so many dismiss the notion of sickness or disease as a punishment from God. "How can you call cancer a judgment from God when innocent children get it?" they might ask. While this is a legitimate question, the intent of the question is misguided. The simple truth is that the Bible is clear on this issue; Exodus 15:26 teaches clearly that disease often comes as God's judgment:

> [God] said, "If you diligently heed the voice of the LORD your God and do what is right in His sight, give ear to His commandments and keep all His statutes, I will put none of the diseases on you which I have brought on the Egyptians. For I am the LORD who heals you."

God clearly declares that the diseases that He brought upon a rebellious Egypt did not have to face His obedient people.

Some Temporal Causes of Sickness (and How to Stay Well)

Lest anyone think this is going to turn into a "diet and wellness book," let's turn to Proverbs to gain insight about staying well and avoiding sickness.

Wrong living can cause disease

> To deliver you from the immoral woman, from the seductress who flatters with her words, who forsakes the companion of her youth, and forgets the covenant of her God. For her house leads down to death, and her paths to the dead; none who go to her return, nor do they regain the paths of life.
> —PROVERBS 2:16-19

It is a simple fact that two people who practice chastity before marriage and fidelity during marriage have zero chance of contracting so many of the sexually transmitted diseases running rampant in our world today. Conversely, a stupid person will practice sexual promiscuity. Let me be clear: there is no such thing as safe sex outside of the confines of the marital bed of two faithful spouses! Today AIDS is killing off entire populations. Obviously, God's plan of one man and one woman for life is the answer. Notice the sad results of sexually transmitted disease.

> For the lips of an immoral woman drip honey, and her mouth is smoother than oil; but in the end she is bitter as wormwood, sharp as a two-edged sword.
> —PROVERBS 5:3-4

> And you mourn at last, when your flesh and your body are consumed, and say: "How I have hated instruction, and my heart despised correction!"
> —PROVERBS 5:11-12

In verses 3 and 4, we see that there is pleasure to be found in immorality. Don't be confused by the metaphor of immorality as a woman; this is a gender-neutral truth—and that pleasure is immediate and very real, but there is a consequence that is also ultimate and just as real. While immorality gives pleasure in its season, the end result is bitterness and division within your spirit.

Live an obedient life

God is a promise-keeping God, and if we would know how to gain the benefits of the blessings He has in store for us, then we must search His Word to know what the promises are. God promises long life to those who live under godly instructions.

> My son, do not forget my law, but let your heart keep my commands; for length of days and long life and peace they will add to you.
>
> —PROVERBS 3:1–2

I think the reason we don't embrace this teaching is because it seems too simple, too antithetical to our current understanding of science and medicine. But if we believe the promises of God are true, we must accept that a focus on God's Word, His law and commands, will not only lengthen our lives but also add peace to our days.

Live trusting in the will of God

> Trust in the LORD with all your heart, and lean not on your own understanding; in all your ways acknowledge Him, and He shall direct your paths. Do not be wise in your own eyes; fear the LORD and depart from evil. It will be health to your flesh, and strength to your bones.
>
> —PROVERBS 3:5–8

"Do not be wise in your own eyes" is a very important directive from God. How often have we held an idea to be true because it seemed "right unto [us], but the end thereof [was] death?" (Prov. 14:12). We cannot trust what seems right to us, but we must compare every idea with Scripture. Here is a direct promise from God for healing when we walk according to His plan for our lives. He calls us to a life of trust.

Learn to receive correction from God

There is a great blessing in having the ability to adjust your lifestyle according to God's correction.

> My son, do not despise the chastening of the LORD, nor detest His correction; for whom the LORD loves He corrects, just as a father the son in whom he delights.
>
> —PROVERBS 3:11–12

The Bible teaches that the father who loves his children will discipline them. We must understand this about our heavenly Father. When we engage in activities that shape our lifestyles in ways that are contrary to what is acceptable in God's sight, there will be—there *must* be—consequences. That doesn't mean that God is angry with us or that He hates us or even that He somehow loves us less; it means only that we are living out the consequence of our choice and experiencing the discipline to be found from the hands of a loving Father who only wishes us to be blessed.

Learn the importance of living wisely

Biblical wisdom is the practical way to live, laid out by God for us all. Wisdom takes knowledge and understanding and makes it simple so that we can act according to its revelation.

> Happy is the man who finds wisdom, and the man who gains understanding; for her proceeds are better than the profits of silver, and her gain than fine gold. She is more precious than rubies, and all the things you may desire cannot compare with her. Length of days is in her right hand, in her left hand riches and honor. Her ways are ways of pleasantness, and all her paths are peace. She is a tree of life to those who take hold of her, and happy are all who retain her.
>
> —Proverbs 3:13–18

Here is the promise of long life, and the truth is that our health is often the result of our own choices in life.

Some Questions

There are those who are born with genetic disorders, physical challenges, and deadly diseases. There are also those who are victims of the crimes of others. There are those caught in times and places of war. God will deal graciously with those who find themselves with such challenges.

While we find it difficult to grasp because of some who do not experience complete healing in this life, we must confess that sickness and evil are not a part of God's perfect will. Because of Adam's fall and man's freedom to choose, we cope with the presence of sickness, disease, and injury.

The Will of God

I have heard people in the face of sickness and death say, "Well, God's will be done." This is an incomplete quote of the Lord's Prayer, which says, "Your will be done on earth as it is in heaven" (Matt. 6:10). God's perfect will is always done in heaven, but it must be transferred to earth by prayer and other spiritual means. In fact, the baptism with the Holy Spirit and His subsequent work is no less than a down payment of the future world. (See my book *An Essential Guide to Baptism of the Holy Spirit.*) Read what Paul wrote in to the church in Ephesus:

> The Spirit is God's guarantee that he will give us the inheritance he promised and that he has purchased us to be his own people. He did this so we would praise and glorify him.
>
> —Ephesians 1:14, nlt

Simply put, evil has resulted in sickness, injury, and death on earth. Our bodies are remnants of Adam's fall and are under the curse of aging and death. The Holy Spirit can bring healing and renewal of our bodies out of the spiritual realm when biblical principles are obeyed.

Therefore, it is God's perfect will that humans live in

health. In forthcoming chapters we will explore healing in the Old Testament, in the life of Christ, in the church today, and in the latter days.

In closing this chapter, let's examine God's declaration—and some scriptural reflections—to the journeying Israelites.

> So you shall serve the LORD your God, and He will bless your bread and your water. And I will take sickness away from the midst of you.
>
> —EXODUS 23:25

> Bless the LORD, O my soul; and all that is within me, bless His holy name! Bless the LORD, O my soul, and forget not all His benefits: who forgives all your iniquities, who heals all your diseases...
>
> —PSALM 103:1–3

> But He was wounded for our transgressions, He was bruised for our iniquities; the chastisement for our peace was upon Him, and by His stripes we are healed.
>
> —ISAIAH 53:5

All of these verses indicate that God's covenant includes healing for all.

> Jesus, keep me near the cross,
> There a precious fountain
> Free to all, a healing stream
> Flows from Calvary's mountain.[2]

CHAPTER THREE
Healing in the Old Testament

EGYPT ENSLAVED THE people of God for four hundred years. God stretched out His mighty hand to rescue His people and to deliver them to a better life. The people stood on the eastern shore of the Red Sea and saw the destruction of Pharaoh's army. This was the final part of judgment after plagues and disease had ravaged Egypt, culminating in the death of the firstborn (sons). The Israelites had been protected by the blood of a lamb on the doorpost. Now out of Egypt, it was God's will that Egypt be taken out of *them*.

Exodus 15 records their journey into the Arabian Peninsula where they were tested at the spring of Marah. *Marah* means "bitter," and its water was undrinkable. Miraculously the water was made drinkable when Moses threw a tree in it. This is a beautiful picture of how Calvary's tree sweetens for us the bitter water of life. God was teaching them faith and faithfulness with this event.

The Covenant of Health

As a result of God's healing the water, He set before them a covenant of healing and health.

> So he cried out to the LORD, and the LORD showed him a tree. When he cast it into the waters, the waters were made sweet. There He made a statute and an ordinance for them, and there He tested them, and said, "If you diligently heed the voice of the LORD your God and do what is right in His sight, give ear to His commandments and keep all His statutes, I will put none of the diseases on you which I have brought on the Egyptians. For I am the LORD who heals you."
>
> —EXODUS 15:25–26

Here were the clear conditions of the healing covenant of God:

1. Be sensitive to the voice of the Lord.
2. Live knowing you are accountable to God.
3. Live in obedience to God's plan for living.
4. Live a life according to God's appointed time.

As I write this, Valentine's Day is approaching, and countless people are sending cards and flowers to their loved ones. These gifts bear declarations such as, "My heart is yours!" or "My heart belongs to you!" The idea conveyed in these sentiments is the sense of faithfulness. They say, "There will be no other for me because all of the love I have to give is in my heart, and my heart is yours!" To "listen carefully to God's voice" means to give God your ear! I find that, more often than not, the reason believers experience a less-than-abundant life is because they have not given their ears fully over to God, but instead they listen to the so-called wisdom of the world and the lies of their enemy. When you do give your ears over to God, you can't hear the negative impact of Satan, this world, or your flesh because your ears *belong to God*!

As you listen to God, the Holy Spirit will instruct you in all things (John 14:26), and as you mature in your faith, you will develop the ability to heed God's commandments. As you submit to God's commandments, you learn to keep God's decrees and to keep appointments made with Him. This includes worship services, appointed meetings and feasts, and faithfulness in giving.

When one lives this way, God makes a covenant of health with the people. First, no disease in Egypt will infect them. Second, God makes a declaration of healing: "For I am the LORD who heals you" (Exod. 15:26).

Here God again declares His covenant name. Moses recognized this as the name given at the burning bush! "I am what I have always been and I am what I will always be…" (author's paraphrase). Yahweh is often translated the great "I AM." Yahweh is the name *Rapha* or "Healer"!

He declares Himself to be Yahweh Rapha (Jehovah Rapha), "the Lord who is Healer."

This combined name means that the Lord is present in the now to heal! His healing was available but conditional upon their faith and obedience in His words. This covenant of healing has never been withdrawn.

Healing as a Benefit of the Old Covenant

David affirms that covenant of healing in Psalm 103.

> He made known His ways to Moses, His acts to the children of Israel.
>
> —PSALM 103:7

God's character and compassion were revealed to Moses. David then composed this song to celebrate the benefits and affirm the covenant of healing in the Lord.

> Bless the LORD, O my soul; and all that is within me, bless His holy name! Bless the LORD, O my soul, and forget not all His benefits: who forgives all your iniquities, who heals all your diseases, who redeems your life from destruction, who crowns you with lovingkindness and tender mercies, who satisfies your mouth with good things, so that your youth is renewed like the eagle's. The LORD executes righteousness and justice for all who are oppressed. He made known His ways to Moses, His acts to the children of Israel.
>
> —PSALM 103:1–7

David explodes in unbridled praise for all of God's goodness. He realizes that the covenant of life and health given to Moses belongs to him. David sets forth a protocol for enjoying the benefits of God's covenant.

1. One's soul, or thinking, has to be right. David called his own soul on the carpet and commanded his thinking to move to praise and thanksgiving. Praise always manifests the presence of God. His presence is essential for receiving benefits. One must never forget God's goodness no matter what the outward circumstance may be.

2. A person must know that their sins are forgiven. Because sin unleashed illness on the earth, forgiveness needs to be received.

3. God heals all diseases. This is an astounding statement! God's desire is for His people to walk in complete health.

4. This leads to a renewed youth, an extended life, and positive lifestyle. All of this moves majestically to David's confession of God's love.

But the mercy of the LORD is from everlasting to everlasting on those who fear Him, and His righteousness to children's children, to such as keep His covenant, and to those who remember His commandments to do them.

—PSALM 103:17–18

God's love and saving power are united together and include healing for those who are faithful to His covenant.

The Promise of the Healing Covenant

The prophets operated in God's healing power. The ministry of Elijah and Elisha are filled with miracles, including healing and raising the dead. God healed the Gentile Naaman of leprosy, extending God's covenant to Gentiles in the Old Testament. Jesus cited this story in Luke 4 and was nearly killed by His own people!

Isaiah the prophet promised a healing Savior.

> Surely He has borne our griefs and carried our sorrows; yet we esteemed Him stricken, smitten by God, and afflicted. But He was wounded for our transgressions, He was bruised for our iniquities; the chastisement for our peace was upon Him, and by His stripes we are healed.
>
> —ISAIAH 53:4–5

The apostle Peter referenced this prophecy in his first letter.

> Who Himself bore our sins in His own body on the tree, that we, having died to sins, might live for righteousness—by whose stripes you were healed.
>
> —1 PETER 2:24

Jeremiah cried out for healing medicine for the people.

> Is there no balm in Gilead, is there no physician
> there? Why then is there no recovery for the health
> of the daughter of my people?
>
> —JEREMIAH 8:22

Malachi spoke of a coming day when the Messiah would bring even greater healing.

> "But to you who fear My name the Sun of
> Righteousness shall arise with healing in His
> wings; and you shall go out and grow fat like
> stall-fed calves. You shall trample the wicked, for
> they shall be ashes under the soles of your feet
> on the day that I do this," says the LORD of hosts.
> "Remember the Law of Moses, My servant, which I
> commanded him in Horeb for all Israel, with the
> statutes and judgments."
>
> —MALACHI 4:2–4

As New Testament Christians, we often overlook the importance and significance of the words given in the Old Testament; we do this at our peril! Notice carefully again that the promised healing is rooted in the covenant with Moses! God, who does not change, has declared, "I am the LORD who heals you" (Exod. 15:26).

CHAPTER FOUR
Jesus the Healer

Jesus Christ spent more time in healing ministry than He did preaching. It is important for you to understand that healing was not an afterthought or add-on to Jesus's ministry. Healing was central to all that He did.

At the inauguration of His ministry Jesus chose Isaiah 61 as His text. Look at Luke's record of that event.

> The Spirit of the Lord is upon Me, because He has anointed Me to preach the gospel to the poor; He has sent Me to heal the brokenhearted, to proclaim liberty to the captives and recovery of sight to the blind, to set at liberty those who are oppressed; to proclaim the acceptable year of the Lord.
>
> —Luke 4:18–19

He followed the announcement by foretelling His own crucifixion and with the stinging rebuke of His hometown by citing two healing miracles by Elijah and Elisha for non-Jews.

> He said to them, "You will surely say this proverb to Me, 'Physician, heal yourself! Whatever we have heard done in Capernaum, do also here in Your country.'" Then He said, "Assuredly, I say to you, no prophet is accepted in his own country. But I tell you truly, many widows were in Israel in the days of Elijah, when the heaven was shut up three years and six months, and there was a great famine throughout all the land; but to none of them was Elijah sent except to Zarephath, in the region of Sidon, to a woman who was a widow. And many lepers were in Israel in the time of Elisha the prophet, and none of them was cleansed except Naaman the Syrian."
>
> —LUKE 4:23–27

The reception of the people was evident. His healing claims were Messianic. In a fury they sought to kill Him.

> So all those in the synagogue, when they heard these things, were filled with wrath, and rose up and thrust Him out of the city; and they led Him to the brow of the hill on which their city was built, that they might throw Him down over the cliff. Then passing through the midst of them, He went His way.
>
> —LUKE 7:28–30

When John the Baptist was jailed and about to be martyred, He inquired of Jesus concerning His role as

Messiah. Jesus's response to John clearly indicates that healing was central in its role of the Messiah on earth.

> And when John had heard in prison about the works of Christ, he sent two of his disciples and said to Him, "Are You the Coming One, or do we look for another?" Jesus answered and said to them, "Go and tell John the things which you hear and see: the blind see and the lame walk; the lepers are cleansed and the deaf hear; the dead are raised up and the poor have the gospel preached to them."
> —MATTHEW 11:2–5

Jesus coming to earth was the breaking through of the kingdom of heaven into the earth. God's great dimension had collided with the cursed, sick, torn world known on earth. Jesus had come to demonstrate through the miracle of healing that a new season had arrived.

Jesus's ministry had this headline: The Kingdom of Heaven Is Here!

> Now after John was put in prison, Jesus came to Galilee, preaching the gospel of the kingdom of God, and saying, "The time is fulfilled, and the kingdom of God is at hand. Repent, and believe in the gospel."
> —MARK 1:14–15

The word *time* is *kairos.* It means "the moment pregnant with promise and opportunity." This special moment included a now king and kingdom. This good news required repentance, a change of mind. The healing miracle of Jesus challenged the limitations of the world, the weakness of the flesh, and the dominion of the devil. Every healing was a blow to Satan's kingdom.

Today this is not the experience in the average church. In the early part of the twentieth century, the strange unbiblical doctrine of cessationism arose and, for the most part, conquered evangelical Christians. The Calvinist scholar Benjamin Breckinridge Warfield declared that "the age of miracles is over."[1] This was popularized in the original Scofield Reference Bible and defended in our present generation by John MacArthur.

Western Christianity is drying up in spiritual anemia and lethargy. The good news Jesus brought released supernatural power that saved the believer and delivered the believer from the kingdom of darkness. Salvation was no less than a rebirth by the spirit from above.

This doctrine has slaughtered faith and left many in helplessness. This lie denies what the Scripture teaches about the unchanging God.

> Jesus Christ is the same yesterday, today, and forever.
>
> —HEBREWS 13:8

Jesus came to release the mighty power of God on earth. His healings gave witness to His person, God the Son. This caused people to receive Him as Lord and

Savior. Today the church must reject the sin of the church of Laodicea. Revelation 3 records the fact that this church had everything *except* Jesus Christ. He was shut out because no one could hear His voice. This church was a growing, prosperous, increasing church with no anointing and power. We must fling open the door to our Christ and allow Him to do His great work again.

Jesus Christ healed and He walked on earth as man. Jesus emptied Himself not of His deity, but of the prerogatives of His deity. He lived on earth as a Spirit-filled man. He left us an example that we should follow in His steps. He promised that the church would do "greater works" than those He did on earth. He declared that the church is His body on earth. Therefore, through the church (His people) the same healing miracles are possible. In fact, He poured out gifts of healing and miracles upon the church.

Let us look at the notable healing miracles of Jesus and how they can be released today.

SECTION TWO

Ten Ways Jesus Healed

CHAPTER FIVE

Jesus Healed by the Word

As WE EXAMINE some notable healings in the life of Christ, we can learn how to release healing in today's church. As His body on earth, we can exercise the same methods for healing that Jesus used.

Among the earliest healings Jesus performed was one in the synagogue at Capernaum.

> And He entered the synagogue again, and a man was there who had a withered hand. So they watched Him closely, whether He would heal him on the Sabbath, so that they might accuse Him. And He said to the man who had the withered hand, "Step forward." Then He said to them, "Is it lawful on the Sabbath to do good or to do evil, to save life or to kill?" But they kept silent. And when He had looked around at them with anger, being grieved by the hardness of their hearts, He said to the man, "Stretch out your hand." And he stretched it out, and his hand was restored as whole as the other. Then the Pharisees went out and immediately plotted with the Herodians against Him, how they might destroy Him.
>
> —MARK 3:1–6

The setting for the miracle was the corporate gathering of God's people for worship. The synagogue would be equivalent to our local churches today. This was not the first time Jesus had been in this place, nor was it the first time this man with the withered hand was before Jesus. Had this man missed a previous opportunity when Jesus had come to minister?

Notice the man's condition. He had a withered hand. The hand represents authority and ability. The word *withered* is a perfect passive in Greek. This means that the man's hand had been injured by something done to this man. He had been injured by a tragic event or an attack. He had not always been without the use of his hand.

There had been good times in the past when that hand had labored profitably, caressed his wife and children, and taken care of many needs. Now it hung useless at his side. He was the victim of some act that was not his doing.

Yet he had not thrown over worship or faith in God because of his misfortune. He came to the synagogue again. When we look at this account, what lesson can we draw about healing today?

1. Healing often takes place where God's people are gathered. I will say more about corporate anointing in a later chapter.

2. Healing only happens when Jesus Christ's presence is experienced. Today, we experience His presence spiritually and through the power of the Holy Spirit.

3. Healing may require public exposure of the need. This man was summoned by Jesus to stand up in the middle of the congregation. All could see his need.

4. The essential truth in this story is what this man is asked to do. Jesus commanded him to "stretch out his hand." That is the word of healing. Here faith must seize this moment and embrace this word.

Being familiar with the Old Testament Scriptures, surely this man could remember the promise made by Yahweh: "He sent His word and healed them" (Ps. 107:20).

This man faced a decision, a crucial moment when he must believe and act on the word, receive or turn away in unbelief. He could not in the natural do what he had been commanded, yet the word of Jesus summoned faith to his soul. As faith laid hold of this word from Jesus, the man's hand was restored as whole as the other. His miracle had been released by the word of Jesus.

Healing can come for you when you are in a congregation that welcomes the presence of Jesus, nurtures faith, and has an atmosphere of expectancy.

The Word of God shall stand,
Shall stand unchanged forever;
In every clime and land
The world shall own its sway.
The Word of God shall stand,

Its foes can change it never;
Though heav'n and earth
May pass away,
God's Word shall stand forever.[1]

CHAPTER SIX
Jesus Healed by Faith

WHAT IS THE greatest example of faith you have ever witnessed? You would expect to discover such faith among the people of God. Jesus made a surprising discovery among the Roman soldiers who were quartered in Israel. Luke gives us this story of healing and faith.

> Now when He concluded all His sayings in the hearing of the people, He entered Capernaum. And a certain centurion's servant, who was dear to him, was sick and ready to die. So when he heard about Jesus, he sent elders of the Jews to Him, pleading with Him to come and heal his servant. And when they came to Jesus, they begged Him earnestly, saying that the one for whom He should do this was deserving, "for he loves our nation, and has built us a synagogue." Then Jesus went with them. And when He was already not far from the house, the centurion sent friends to Him, saying to Him, "Lord, do not trouble Yourself, for I am not worthy that You should enter under my roof. Therefore I did not even think myself worthy to come to You.

But say the word, and my servant will be healed. For I also am a man placed under authority, having soldiers under me. And I say to one, 'Go,' and he goes; and to another, 'Come,' and he comes; and to my servant, 'Do this,' and he does it." When Jesus heard these things, He marveled at him, and turned around and said to the crowd that followed Him, "I say to you, I have not found such great faith, not even in Israel!" And those who were sent, returning to the house, found the servant well who had been sick.

—LUKE 7:1–10

Religious people can be disappointing at times. Jesus found little faith among His people. Yet a Roman officer received the honor of being the greatest person of faith during Jesus's earthly ministry.

As enemies of Israel, Roman soldiers were unwelcome. Yet an exception was found in the Galilean village of Capernaum. The Jews of that city bore witness to Jesus of this man's character. The Roman had a servant whom he was very fond of who had grown deathly ill. He needed healing. Immediately the fact that this Roman cared about those who worked for him speaks of his character. Second, the leader of the local synagogue respected him and begged Jesus to help him. Third, they bore witness that he loved the nation of Israel. Fourth, he had paid for and had constructed their house of worship! Here was a unique layman: a soldier of an invading nation came in and embraced the religion and faith of the conquered so much so that he funded, solely, a local house of worship, and yet today Christians everywhere argue over whether or not they should tithe or give monetary offerings at all to their church!

What qualified this man for favor with Jesus? Let me suggest four favor-releasing actions that this man exhibited.

1. He had mercy on the hurting. Jesus promised blessing on the merciful!

2. He respected the anointed elder over the place he lived. Though a high-ranking officer, he submitted to the spiritual authority of the Jewish elders.

3. He loved the nation of Israel. God had promised blessing on those that bless Israel (Gen. 12:1–3).

4. He had built God a house!

God gives favor to those who provide a place for Him to be worshiped. This man's *entire life* was a memorial before God that released double blessings and favor.

After hearing the testimony of the elders of Israel, Jesus went with them to this man. Immediately, the Roman called Jesus "Lord." His own faith had embraced Jesus while many had rejected Him. He threw himself and the need of his dying servant on the grace of Jesus, declaring his own unworthiness. He then made the greatest faith confession in the four Gospels. As an officer under the authority of Rome he could take orders and give orders. These orders would be carried out whether he was present or not! Understanding the authority of Jesus, the Roman said to Him, "Say the word and my servant will be healed."

Here was a man who grasped the power of the word from Jesus's mouth! He understood the force of faith that went with that word. He saw that Jesus was not limited by a building, a ritual, a certain race, or a certain time. This man had great faith that when Jesus declared it, it would be done.

The truth is that Jesus simply released the Roman's faith, and that healed the servant. Curiosity seekers went and checked, and soon the reports came that the man was well.

What Is Great Faith?

The greatest faith needs no sign, no religious hocus pocus, no certain person, simply Jesus. You see, faith is believing and acting on what Jesus has promised as if it is so when it does not seem so, until it is so!

Faith draws on the invisible resources of the kingdom and moves them to a life situation. Faith is not simply a feeling. Faith confesses the promise of Jesus no matter the circumstances or feelings.

Why was this Roman commander's faith great? He did not require hands-on ministry, anointing oil, prayer cloths, or a special healing service. All he needed was Jesus's word, and he believed. Contrast this to Jairus, the president of the synagogue who required Jesus to come to his house, or think of Mary and Martha who were angry because Jesus did not come quickly to their brother's aid.

Understand that the greatest faith comes when you put no limit on the authority and word of the Lord Jesus. This "word of faith" is first "in your mouth" and then "in your heart" (Rom. 10:8). This man simply said to Jesus, "Give the order and it will be done." This is raw, naked, and unyielding faith, with all the religious jargon and trappings stripped away. Here is faith that stretches across oceans, moves mountains, brings prodigals home, and heals our sick friends.

Great faith flows out of a heart of character, of caring, and of covenant! Do you want someone healed? Come to Jesus, loving His people and believing His word!

CHAPTER SEVEN
Jesus Healed to Release Service

W HY DOES GOD heal? He heals because of His mercy, because of covenant, because of His Word, and in response to faith. This is what we have observed thus far, but sometimes God's healing grace is extended for less dramatic reasons. We observe that in Jesus's visit to minister at the synagogue at Capernaum.

Capernaum was hometown to Simon Peter. Archeologists have uncovered the foundation of his home. Peter's wife's mother lived in the home with them. Jesus and some of His followers had gone to synagogue on the Sabbath. While there, Jesus had cast a demon out of a man. It was a dramatic and amazing moment.

> Now there was a man in their synagogue with an unclean spirit. And he cried out, saying, "Let us alone! What have we to do with You, Jesus of Nazareth? Did You come to destroy us? I know who You are—the Holy One of God!" But Jesus rebuked him, saying, "Be quiet, and come out of him!" And when the unclean spirit had convulsed him and cried out with a loud voice, he came out of him.

> Then they were all amazed, so that they questioned among themselves, saying, "What is this? What new doctrine is this? For with authority He commands even the unclean spirits, and they obey Him."
>
> —Mark 1:23–27

Imagine the intensity of this moment of deliverance and healing. Imagine a possessed man jumping up in the middle of your church service, screaming and disrupting the proceedings. How would you respond? How would you expect your deacons, your elders, or your pastors to respond? Note how Jesus responded: seven words spoken "with *authority*"!

After the service Jesus went home with Simon Peter. Being the Sabbath, the meal had been prepared the day before and wrapped in such a way to keep it warm because no fire would be kindled on the Sabbath. All of them were expecting to eat.

Upon arriving at the home, they found Peter's mother-in-law sick with a high fever. Look at the record of Scripture:

> But Simon's wife's mother lay sick with a fever, and they told Him about her at once. So He came and took her by the hand and lifted her up, and immediately the fever left her. And she served them.
>
> —Mark 1:30–31

They informed Jesus that the family matriarch was very sick. Notice the setting for this miracle is in the home. Again we learn that healing is not circumscribed by any particular setting. In this account, Jesus simply takes her hand and helps her sit up. There is no word, no faith mentioned; simply, a loving assist by Jesus to sit up. Jesus's compassionate touch released healing and immediately the fever left her!

Interestingly, she gets up and serves the Sabbath meal she had prepared the day before! She is healed and strong. The word *serve* comes from the Greek word *diakonos*, from which our English word *deacon* comes. The word means "through the dust." It means to move so quickly into service that one kicks up some dust. This dear woman was able to resume work and exercise the gift of hospitality for Jesus and her family.

It is touching to me that Mark would take note of the fact that she served them a meal. Jesus remembered her kindness, and it is recorded for us today. For a Jewish woman, hospitality was an important part of her life. In Jewish culture there was a protocol of hospitality required by Scripture. This woman's fever kept her from rendering the service she wanted to give to Jesus. Jesus's healing released her to serve in her gifting. In all of our service to Jesus, whether we feel it is great or small, we can ask for healing in order to arise and serve our Master.

I further think that there is a picture of corporate healing for the church. Our churches have grown anemic and sick while a hungry world awaits what we have prepared that they so desperately need. It is clear that Jesus healed to release service!

CHAPTER EIGHT
Jesus Healed to Restore Life

L EPROSY WAS THE cancer or AIDS of Jesus's day.
This disease was a slow, excruciating death. Gradually, this highly infectious disease consumed the flesh, caused digits to fall off, and crippled and incapacitated its victims. Furthermore, those so afflicted were cut off from society and family. They had to live outside the normal social circles. There was no known cure for this disease. There are several accounts of Jesus healing this incurable disease. Mark records the first such encounter:

> Now a leper came to Him, imploring Him, kneeling down to Him and saying to Him, "If You are willing, You can make me clean." Then Jesus, moved with compassion, stretched out His hand and touched him, and said to him, "I am willing; be cleansed." As soon as He had spoken, immediately the leprosy left him, and he was cleansed. And He strictly warned him and sent him away at once, and said to him, "See that you say nothing to anyone; but go your way, show yourself to the priest, and offer for your cleansing those things which Moses commanded, as a testimony to

them." However, he went out and began to proclaim it freely, and to spread the matter, so that
Jesus could no longer openly enter the city, but was
outside in deserted places; and they came to Him
from every direction.

—MARK 1:40–45

How far are you willing to go to be healed? Here a man
with leprosy falls at the feet of Jesus, begging to be healed.
He knew no shame, but on his knees he begged for favor
from Jesus. Those who spurn outward expressions of ministry such as laying on of hands, anointing with oil, being
slain in the Spirit, kneeling, and weeping loudly ought to
be careful. Perhaps those who ridicule such expressions
have never stared consumptive disease and painful death
in the face!

I recall my own heart incident and the apprehension it
brought to me. As I lay wired up in intensive care, I felt
alone. At midnight a nurse came in and offered to anoint
me with oil and pray over me in tongues. I replied, "Pour
the whole bottle of oil on me; pray in every way you know
how!" God heard those prayers and my heart was healed.
There is something about desperation that touches Jesus
in His innermost soul. Here is a desperate man who sees
Jesus as his last hope for life.

This cry caused Jesus to be "moved with compassion."
In the original Greek it is a passive verb form (or an aorist),
which means something inside that man pulled out Jesus's
innermost being!

I believe it was the simple request with which the man begged Jesus for healing. Verse 40 records the poignant moment. "If You are willing, You can make me clean." The word *can* is from *dunamis*, which is "miracle-working power." Literally, the man says to Jesus, "If it is Your will, then I know You have the miracle-working power to heal me."

Jesus responds with a simple act and a saving, healing word. He touches the leper, which violated the tradition of religion and broke the laws of hygiene. By touching this leper Jesus was willing to take on his disease.

Then Jesus said, "I am willing." In Greek that statement is in the present active indicative tense, which means "I go on being willing to heal." I have heard people say they want to be healed "if it's God's will." This settles that question. Healing goes on being the will of our Lord Jesus Christ!

It is very clear that Jesus responded to this man's heart-felt cry for healing. Obviously, many lepers were not healed in Israel during Jesus's day. I wonder how many were willing to take the risk and come publicly and beg for what they needed! Something in this man grabbed hold of Jesus's heart, and compassion healed this man.

Today, compassion for the terminal will still move the heart of God. First it must move the heart of the people of God. Let us settle the question forever about healing. Jesus said, "I am willing."

CHAPTER NINE

Jesus Healed Through the Faith of Others

I HAVE OFTEN HEARD that people are not healed because of their own lack of faith. While one's faith can release healing, some who have no record of faith are healed. Healing cannot be conformed to one method or approach. There is an incident of healing early in Jesus's ministry that defies traditional thought.

> And again He entered Capernaum after some days, and it was heard that He was in the house. Immediately many gathered together, so that there was no longer room to receive them, not even near the door. And He preached the word to them. Then they came to Him, bringing a paralytic who was carried by four men. And when they could not come near Him because of the crowd, they uncovered the roof where He was. So when they had broken through, they let down the bed on which the paralytic was lying. When Jesus saw their faith, He said to the paralytic, "Son, your sins are forgiven you." And some of the scribes were sitting there and reasoning in their hearts, "Why does this Man speak blasphemies

like this? Who can forgive sins but God alone?"
But immediately, when Jesus perceived in His
spirit that they reasoned thus within themselves,
He said to them, "Why do you reason about these
things in your hearts? Which is easier, to say to
the paralytic, 'Your sins are forgiven you,' or to say,
'Arise, take up your bed and walk'? But that you
may know that the Son of Man has power on earth
to forgive sins"—He said to the paralytic, "I say to
you, arise, take up your bed, and go to your house."
Immediately he arose, took up the bed, and went
out in the presence of them all, so that all were
amazed and glorified God, saying, "We never saw
anything like this!"

—MARK 2:1–12

In this account the home where Jesus is staying in
Capernaum is crowded with people expecting ministry from
Jesus. This place was packed and no one could get in. Jesus
was preaching the Word of God to them. It is noteworthy
that preaching the Word preceded hands-on ministry.

Jesus's preaching was interrupted as roof tiles were
lifted away and a physically challenged man was lowered
by ropes on a pallet in front of Jesus.

There is no record that this man wanted to be there.
There is no record that his own faith brought him there.
What we do see is a group of men with the audacity to get
their friend to Jesus at all costs. Their kind of love spared

no effort or expense to see loved ones come to Christ to have their need met.

I preached on this text one Sunday years ago, and after the service my most ornery deacon asked, "I wonder who had to pay for the roof?" What an attitude! How sad when we are more worried about our order or our cost more than a lost, sick, and hurting person!

It took four men to carry this man to Jesus! Each one had to carry his share of the load. Yet their cooperation got him to the desired destination.

What released healing to the life of this man? What gave him back his legs? It is clear in verse 5: "Jesus saw their faith." The faith of these four men brought healing and salvation to their friend!

Critics overheard Jesus say to the paralyzed man, "Your sins are forgiven you…" Jesus wanted this man to know that the presence of sin on the earth came from Satan, that sin released sickness, and that forgiveness opened the door to healing!

Immediately, the critics recognized in Jesus's remarks His valid claim to deity. Jesus proved His right to forgive by healing the man. Before the eyes of His critics the man leaped to his feet and walked out. The stunned observers were amazed!

The important thing to note here is that the daring faith of one's friends can get them healed.

CHAPTER TEN
Jesus Healed Through Deliverance

MEDICAL AUTHORITIES AFFIRM that much of our sicknesses begin in our mind. Our mental state often determines our level of health. Add to that the operation of demonic spirits on one's mental state, and it is clear that mental oppression is a great need in healing ministry.

A young man in our church tells the story of the first time he encountered a demonic spirit:

> It was during the "altar call" portion of the service, and I had been praying for people when someone asked me to come pray for a woman who had remained seated the entire time. As I walked over to her, I felt something unusual; I was fairly new to all of this, so I didn't think anything of it at the time. I looked down at the woman who had to have been five feet nothing and about one hundred pounds. Her arms and legs were crossed so tightly she might have been made from marble.
>
> I knelt down in front of her and placed my hands on her head and began to pray for her.

Quite suddenly, I found it difficult to speak. I opened my eyes and looked at this woman's face, and her eyes were as black and empty as anything I had ever seen. All of a sudden I began to have trouble breathing. I tried to stand and couldn't. People were helping me stand when she lashed out and started screaming and flailing her arms all over.

As I stood to the side trying to breathe, I saw another man begin to pray over her trying to cast out whatever it was inside her. She was fighting and screaming and, quite honestly, scaring me to death! A man lay his hand on her and she fell but was bending and contorting as she lay on the floor. He was screaming the name of Jesus over her, but, to my dismay, it seemed to be doing no good.

Then I saw the associate pastor coming down the aisle looking almost like he was strolling through the park. He approached the scene and told the man to stop. The woman lay on the ground still. The pastor said to her, "Stop that! In Jesus' name, leave her alone now. She's had enough." He didn't scream. There were no dynamic motions or flailing of hands. He simply spoke with authority and whatever that was in her was gone.

Immediately, I began to breathe easy again.[1]

Demonic spirits can plant thoughts, tempt, oppress, and depress believers. They can also bring physical infirmity upon believers. Jesus's ministry to the demonically affected was called healing.

> God anointed Jesus of Nazareth with the Holy
> Spirit and with power, who went about doing good
> and healing all who were oppressed by the devil,
> for God was with Him.
>
> —ACTS 10:38

Jesus healed "all" who were oppressed by demonic powers. When we begin to examine the New Testament, we discover those who had lost sight and speech because of demonic oppression (Matt. 12:22–37). We discover suicidal young people affected by demons (Matt. 17:14–21). We discover a woman whose back had been bowed over for decades was afflicted by a spirit of infirmity (Luke 13:10–17). All of these were healed by *evicting* the demon!

Perhaps the worst case is found in Mark 5. Here is a man we would call insane.

> Then they came to the other side of the sea, to
> the country of the Gadarenes. And when He
> had come out of the boat, immediately there met
> Him out of the tombs a man with an unclean
> spirit, who had his dwelling among the tombs;
> and no one could bind him, not even with chains,
> because he had often been bound with shackles
> and chains. And the chains had been pulled
> apart by him, and the shackles broken in pieces;
> neither could anyone tame him. And always,
> night and day, he was in the mountains and in
> the tombs, crying out and cutting himself with
> stones.

When he saw Jesus from afar, he ran and worshiped Him. And he cried out with a loud voice and said, "What have I to do with You, Jesus, Son of the Most High God? I implore You by God that You do not torment me."

For He said to him, "Come out of the man, unclean spirit!" Then He asked him, "What is your name?" And he answered, saying, "My name is Legion; for we are many." Also he begged Him earnestly that He would not send them out of the country.

Now a large herd of swine was feeding there near the mountains. So all the demons begged Him, saying, "Send us to the swine, that we may enter them." And at once Jesus gave them permission. Then the unclean spirits went out and entered the swine (there were about two thousand); and the herd ran violently down the steep place into the sea, and drowned in the sea.

So those who fed the swine fled, and they told it in the city and in the country. And they went out to see what it was that had happened. Then they came to Jesus, and saw the one who had been demon-possessed and had the legion, sitting and clothed and in his right mind. And they were afraid. And those who saw it told them how it happened to him who had been demon-possessed, and about the swine.

Then they began to plead with Him to depart from their region. And when He got into the boat,

he who had been demon-possessed begged Him
that he might be with Him. However, Jesus did
not permit him, but said to him, "Go home to your
friends, and tell them what great things the Lord
has done for you, and how He has had compassion
on you." And he departed and began to proclaim
in Decapolis all that Jesus had done for him; and
all marveled.

—MARK 5:1–20

As you read the account it is obvious that demons have
sickened this man mentally so much that he is incapable
of normal living. He has lost self-control. He lives in agony
and rage. He cuts his own body in self-hate. He is considered dangerous to society, and efforts have been made
to chain him. He has demonstrated inordinate strength
by breaking his bonds. He has also lost every sense of
decency by living naked in a graveyard.

Before we judge this man too harshly, look at our own
day. It is evident that our jails and even our society are full
of people who murder, rape, and terrorize others.

Why is it we see this naked man as strange and yet
laugh at young college women in a wet T-shirt contest?
The pornography industry is full of demonized victims.

What can be done for those whose lives have become
a habitation of demonic spirits? They must meet Jesus.
Healing for those who are demonically affected must
begin with deliverance. You cannot counsel out what
must be cast out. These unfortunate people need the

help of others to pray them through to freedom. (See my book *Everyone's Guide to Demons and Spiritual Warfare.*)

When Jesus finished with this man, he was clothed and in his right mind. He was ready to go home to his family and rejoin society.

The church must embrace deliverance as a means of healing today. So many bound in oppression could live in freedom if we would walk them through this need in their lives.

CHAPTER ELEVEN
Jesus Healed the Desperate

AFTER DELIVERING THE possessed as mentioned in the previous chapter, Jesus crossed the sea and was met by Jairus, the leader of the local synagogue, who had a daughter near death. Jairus fell at Jesus's feet and begged Him to come heal the little girl. On the way there, Jesus had a strange encounter with a woman.

> Now a certain woman had a flow of blood for twelve years, and had suffered many things from many physicians. She had spent all that she had and was no better, but rather grew worse. When she heard about Jesus, she came behind Him in the crowd and touched His garment. For she said, "If only I may touch His clothes, I shall be made well."
>
> Immediately the fountain of her blood was dried up, and she felt in her body that she was healed of the affliction. And Jesus, immediately knowing in Himself that power had gone out of Him, turned around in the crowd and said, "Who touched My clothes?"
>
> But His disciples said to Him, "You see the

multitude thronging You, and You say, 'Who touched Me?'" And He looked around to see her who had done this thing. But the woman, fearing and trembling, knowing what had happened to her, came and fell down before Him and told Him the whole truth. And He said to her, "Daughter, your faith has made you well. Go in peace, and be healed of your affliction."

—MARK 5:25–34

Many were thronging Jesus as He made His way to Jairus's house, yet only one who touched Him got healed. This person is identified as a "certain woman," which means she was known to all in the town. She was afflicted with a female disease that caused her to bleed constantly. Because of this condition she was cut off from her family, her synagogue, and all of society. She was considered unclean.

Under the law, "this blood discharge" rendered the woman as unclean as a leper. (See Numbers 5:2.) Furthermore, it seems that hers was the result of a disease. It is possible that she had contracted a venereal disease that was incurable. Such diseases have followed armies through the centuries. Whether or not this was true, her affliction destroyed her reputation completely.

It is likely that Jairus was her rabbi, and he was head of the synagogue. It is also interesting that his daughter is the same age as the years this woman had been ill.

In her illness and desperation, she offended every

social and religious protocol and broke through the crowd to touch the hem of Jesus's garment. Undoubtedly this would have been the fringe or tzitzit of Jesus's talit or prayer shawl. We know He had it on because later He would wrap Jairus's daughter in it.

> Then He took the child by the hand, and said to her, "Talitha, cumi," which is translated, "Little girl, I say to you, arise."
>
> —MARK 5:41

Notice the words *"Talitha, cumi."* In a conversation with Rabbi Curt Landry, we discussed this text and discovered something amazing. The ancient Hebrew word *tal* meant "covering," with the idea of being covered as with dew. It was often used to reference a tent or tabernacle. This word evolved into the Aramaic word *tal*, which meant "lamb," from the Hebrew word *talaw*, which meant to cover with pieces or, more specifically, a covering for a lamb. So we have this word *tal* as the beginning of *talit* or prayer shawl worn by Jesus. *Talitha, cumi* then is a play on words. Jesus says, figuratively, "Little one in My talit, I say arise."

So we have before us in this story a desperate woman who is considered incurable who seizes her moment and touches Jesus.

Jesus Knows Who Is Desperate

In this story, as we have said, many crowded around Him and touched Him, but only one was healed by His touch.

In the miraculous moment Jesus asked, "Who touched me?" (See Mark 5:30.) The disciples were astounded, seeing the great crowds around Him.

Jesus knew that power had been drawn from Him. Somebody's touch was different. What had happened? Simply put: desperation mixed with faith places a demand upon the anointing!

This woman came before Jesus and fell trembling before Him, knowing she was instantly healed! Note also that she "told Him the whole truth."

You see, she had a story! We do not know how she came to be diseased, but she knew she could confess her story to Jesus. The truth set her free and Jesus changed her identity! At the beginning of this story she was just another sick, dying woman. When it ends, Jesus says to her, "Daughter…" She is now in the family with a new destiny. She can go in peace, for Jesus has set her free from her past.

Sometimes when we want healing, we must be willing to take desperate measures to get to Jesus. All pride must be broken, and we must tell Him the whole truth!

CHAPTER TWELVE
Jesus Healed the Persistent

A WOMAN OF TYRE and Sidon confronted Jesus upon His arrival in her country.

And behold, a woman of Canaan came from that region and cried out to Him, saying, "Have mercy on me, O Lord, Son of David! My daughter is severely demon-possessed."

But He answered her not a word. And His disciples came and urged Him, saying, "Send her away, for she cries out after us."

But He answered and said, "I was not sent except to the lost sheep of the house of Israel."

Then she came and worshiped Him, saying, "Lord, help me!"

But He answered and said, "It is not good to take the children's bread and throw it to the little dogs."

And she said, "Yes, Lord, yet even the little dogs eat the crumbs which fall from their masters' table."

Then Jesus answered and said to her, "O woman,

great is your faith! Let it be to you as you desire."
And her daughter was healed from that very hour.

—MATTHEW 15:22–28

The Greek text indicates that she was screaming noisily at Jesus and the disciples. Her actions were disturbing and disruptive. The disciples wanted Jesus to send her away. She was out of control and also not a Jew.

Jesus simply ignored the woman. Can you imagine someone approaching a pastor today and simply being ignored? Jesus did not say a word. Finally, due to her refusal to take no for an answer, Jesus spoke to her rather rudely.

"I was not sent except to the lost sheep of the house of Israel" (Matt. 15:24).

Now this statement did two things. One, it confirmed the racial tension that was in that land then and remains today. Second, it required this Phoenician woman to embrace a Jewish Messiah!

She called him "Lord" and continued to beg for help.

Dog food and healing

Jesus then insulted the Gentile woman with this statement, "It is not good to take the children's bread and throw it to the little dogs" (Matt. 15:26).

He called the woman and her child dogs! Now, this was the common term for non-Jews in that time. They were called Gentile dogs.

Persistence pays off

This woman refused to be put off even by a racial slur and insult. "And she said, 'Yes, Lord, yet even the little dogs eat the crumbs which fall from their masters' table.'" (Matt. 15:27). Her response indicated a great faith. Jesus recognized that faith and healed her daughter instantly.

To be healed often means to wait on God's timing and not to give up or be put off. God may strip you of your pride in order to expose your persistent faith. Great faith is faith that does not quit!

CHAPTER THIRTEEN

Jesus Healed to Reveal the Heart of God

ONE OF THE most fascinating healing accounts in the Gospels is the healing of the blind man in John 9. Jesus and His followers were discussing a man born blind. The disciples wanted to know whose sin caused the sickness. Jesus debunked the tradition, popular in His day, that all sickness was caused by someone's sin. Jesus told them that God had permitted the blindness in order to bring revelation knowledge of the work of God. It is critical that you understand that healing is "a work of God." He still heals to reveal His kingdom or His nature.

Spit and Mud

Sometimes Jesus worked in ways that were messy and difficult to understand. Consider the case of the blind man found in John 9. Jesus was confronted by His disciples who wanted to know whose sin was responsible for the man's blindness: his sins or his parents' sins. Jesus told them that this man had been afflicted so that God's glory could be revealed in his healing. Here, Jesus makes the great declaration He is "the light of the world." (John 9:5)

Jesus then spits on the ground and makes an anointing of mud and spittle. He anoints the man's eyes with this concoction and sends him to wash in the pool of Siloam. The man obeyed and came back seeing (John 9:6–7)!

Here was clear revelation of God's works and Jesus's messiahship. Yet, what follows is a comedy of investigation.

> Therefore [his neighbors] said to him, "How were your eyes opened?"
>
> He answered and said, "A Man called Jesus made clay and anointed my eyes and said to me, 'Go to the pool of Siloam and wash.' So I went and washed, and I received sight."
>
> Then they said to him, "Where is He?"
>
> He said, "I do not know."
>
> —JOHN 9:10–12

Notice his neighbors asked and he told them exactly what happened. Not believing, they brought him to the religious intelligentsia.

> They brought him who formerly was blind to the Pharisees. Now it was a Sabbath when Jesus made the clay and opened his eyes. Then the Pharisees also asked him again how he had received his sight. He said to them, "He put clay on my eyes, and I washed, and I see."
>
> Therefore some of the Pharisees said, "This Man is not from God, because He does not keep the Sabbath." Others said, "How can a man who is

a sinner do such signs?" And there was a division among them.

They said to the blind man again, "What do you say about Him because He opened your eyes?"

He said, "He is a prophet." But the Jews did not believe concerning him, that he had been blind and received his sight, until they called the parents of him who had received his sight.

—JOHN 9:13–18

Here, they argue with the blind man and call his parents. They make it clear that he is their son and that he was born blind. They were afraid, however, of being put out of the synagogue.

And they asked them, saying, "Is this your son, who you say was born blind? How then does he now see?"

His parents answered them and said, "We know that this is our son, and that he was born blind; but by what means he now sees we do not know, or who opened his eyes we do not know. He is of age; ask him. He will speak for himself." His parents said these things because they feared the Jews, for the Jews had agreed already that if anyone confessed that He was Christ, he would be put out of the synagogue. Therefore his parents said, "He is of age; ask him."

—JOHN 9:19–23

Again, they call the healed man and question him and he gives this classic response:

> He answered and said, "Whether He is a sinner or not I do not know. One thing I know: that though I was blind, now I see."
>
> —John 9:25

Still, they persist in questioning the miracle and he responds:

> Then they said to him again, "What did He do to you? How did He open your eyes?"
>
> He answered them, "I told you already, and you did not listen. Why do you want to hear it again? Do you also want to become His disciples?"
>
> Then they reviled him and said, "You are His disciple, but we are Moses' disciples. We know that God spoke to Moses; as for this fellow, we do not know where He is from."
>
> The man answered and said to them, "Why, this is a marvelous thing, that you do not know where He is from; yet He has opened my eyes! Now we know that God does not hear sinners; but if anyone is a worshiper of God and does His will, He hears him. Since the world began it has been unheard of that anyone opened the eyes of one who was born blind. If this Man were not from God, He could do nothing."
>
> They answered and said to him, "You were

completely born in sins, and are you teaching us?"
And they cast him out.

—John 9:26–34

Finally, as a reward for accepting his healing and answering their questions truthfully, they cast him out of the synagogue.

Healing Disturbs the Status Quo

Here is a man who was cast out of his synagogue (the equivalent of a church) because Jesus healed him. Jesus works will not be controlled, confined, or restricted by man's religion or parameters.

Jesus used spit and mud to heal this man; that way only God could get the glory. God will heal through unusual means to release revelation of His mighty works.

CHAPTER FOURTEEN
Jesus Healed His Enemies

WHEN THE ROMANS came to arrest Jesus, an enraged Peter pulled out a sword and cut off the ear of the high priest's servant Malchus. Luke recorded this story.

> When those around Him saw what was going to happen, they said to Him, "Lord, shall we strike with the sword?" And one of them struck the servant of the high priest and cut off his right ear.
> But Jesus answered and said, "Permit even this." And He touched his ear and healed him.
> —LUKE 22:49–51

According to Josephus, Malchus was a slave of the high priest (*Antiquities* 14:13). Whatever the cause, Jesus healed the ear by a restorative miracle. We have no record or history of what happened to Malchus. We do know that the healing was genuine because Luke, the doctor, recorded the incident for us. Also, it was Jesus's last miracle before the cross.

The point is that sometimes Jesus heals just to relieve

human suffering. In this brief account we learn that Jesus's healing power cannot be limited even by racial or social barriers. Jesus took compassion on this poor slave and healed him. Note that there was no faith, no church connection, no praise, no worship, and no reason for this man to be healed.

Jesus revealed that healing is His sovereign will and choice! So, this healing miracle leaves us without a doctrine of healing, but with simply a Lord who heals whom He will. He is sovereign!

It is critically important for us to understand that signs and wonders, especially healing, open the eyes of the lost. In the Muslim world, nothing brings converts like miracles! Such signs were to follow all believers in their witness around the world (Mark 16:17). Jesus set the example not only in this story but also in the healing of the blind man in John before He, Jesus, saved him.

We should not hesitate to release healing ministry to those who are not yet followers of Jesus.

SECTION THREE

Healing Through Today's Church

CHAPTER FIFTEEN
Healing Ministry in the Body of Christ Today

HEALING IS ONE of the most controversial subjects one can raise in the church. Without a doubt, the Bible is filled with miracles of healing. Further, it seems clear that healing is a by-product of the stripes Jesus endured before the cross.

> But He was wounded for our transgressions, he was bruised for our iniquities; the chastisement for our peace was upon Him, and by His stripes we are healed.
>
> —ISAIAH 53:5

> When evening had come, they brought to Him many who were demon-possessed. And He cast out the spirits with a word, and healed all who were sick, that it might be fulfilled which was spoken by Isaiah the prophet, saying: "He Himself took our infirmities and bore our sicknesses."
>
> —MATTHEW 8:16–17

> Who Himself bore our sins in His own body on
> the tree, that we, having died to sins, might live for
> righteousness—by whose stripes you were healed.
> —1 PETER 2:24

Furthermore, the early church experienced miracles of healing as well. In fact, health and prosperity were objects of prayer.

> Beloved, I pray that you may prosper in all things
> and be in health, just as your soul prospers.
> —3 JOHN 2

Looking at the healing ministry of Jesus, the church must recognize that we are His body on earth today. Therefore, we must exhibit the same passion for healing that we have observed. Note the following about Jesus's healing miracles.

Jesus healed:

- By the Word
- By the faith of the sick
- To release service
- To restore life
- Through the faith of others
- To deliver from demons
- The desperate

- ♦ The persistent
- ♦ To reveal God (and God's heart)
- ♦ His enemies

Therefore the church must release His healing power to our generation.

But What About...?

Knowing all of this, there are still questions and controversy that swirl around ministries of healing.

1. Does God heal all?
2. Why are some not healed?
3. Whose faith is necessary? The sick? The minister? Both?

I want to confess that I don't know all the answers, but I have searched Scripture so I can know how God healed. I have found ten ways the church can release God's healing power.

1. The presence of the gifting and anointing to heal

There are times when God releases the gifts of healing in certain places. The anointing is so great that even clothes are used as points of contact. People are healed in a Spirit-saturated environment where gifts of healing are released.

> Now God worked unusual miracles by the hands
> of Paul, so that even handkerchiefs or aprons were
> brought from his body to the sick, and the diseases
> left them and the evil spirits went out of them.
>
> —ACTS 19:11–12

> …to another faith by the same Spirit, to another
> gifts of healings by the same Spirit…
>
> —1 CORINTHIANS 12:9

Clearly, healing is a gift given for the benefit of the
church and for the glory of God.

2. The laying on of hands

It is the privilege of every true believer to lay hands on
the sick and pray for their recovery. There is a "body life"
and a spiritual transference that takes place in the invisible
realm.

> They will take up serpents; and if they drink any-
> thing deadly, it will by no means hurt them; they
> will lay hands on the sick, and they will recover.
>
> —MARK 16:18

3. Elders, prayer, and the anointing oil

> Is anyone among you sick? Let him call for the
> elders of the church, and let them pray over him,
> anointing him with oil in the name of the Lord.
>
> —JAMES 5:14

Here the believer by his own volition calls for the pastors. Confession of sin and heart preparation is necessary. The oil symbolizes the work of the Holy Spirit.

4. Speaking the Word to your sickness

> For assuredly, I say to you, whoever says to this mountain, "Be removed and be cast into the sea," and does not doubt in his heart, but believes that those things he says will be done, he will have whatever he says.
>
> —MARK 11:23

Note carefully that the believer must say clearly his need. This word must be spoken confidently. Here is a tool to keep using until the sickness leaves!

5. The power of agreement and healing

> Again I say to you that if two of you agree on earth concerning anything that they ask, it will be done for them by My Father in heaven. For where two or three are gathered together in My name, I am there in the midst of them.
>
> —MATTHEW 18:19–20

The reason God gave us the church was so that we could learn the power of agreement. Psalm 133 speaks of God's commanded blessing when two or more get into agreement about the will of God.

You need a church to come into agreement with you for your healing.

6. Your own faith

> Therefore I say to you, whatever things you ask when you pray, believe that you receive them, and you will have them.
>
> —Mark 11:24

Your own faith-saturated prayer can deliver healing to you. Faith will make plans and move on in spite of the sickness.

7. The name of Jesus

> And whatever you ask in My name, that I will do, that the Father may be glorified in the Son. If you ask anything in My name, I will do it.
>
> —John 14:13–14

The name of Jesus is a powerful force against disease and devils. It is a veritable battering ram knocking down the disease.

> Now Peter and John went up together to the temple at the hour of prayer, the ninth hour. And a certain man lame from his mother's womb was carried, whom they laid daily at the gate of the temple which is called Beautiful, to ask alms from those who entered the temple; who, seeing Peter

and John about to go into the temple, asked for alms. And fixing his eyes on him, with John, Peter said, "Look at us." So he gave them his attention, expecting to receive something from them.

Then Peter said, "Silver and gold I do not have, but what I do have I give you: In the name of Jesus Christ of Nazareth, rise up and walk." And he took him by the right hand and lifted him up, and immediately his feet and ankle bones received strength. So he, leaping up, stood and walked and entered the temple with them—walking, leaping, and praising God.

—ACTS 3:1–8

Notice it was the name of Jesus that brought healing.

8. Praying for others

And the LORD restored Job's losses when he prayed for his friends. Indeed the LORD gave Job twice as much as he had before.

—JOB 42:10

God brought total restoration to Job when he forgot self-interest and began to intercede for his wayward friends. In the midst of his intercession God gave him what he needed.

9. The faith of others

> When Jesus saw their faith, He said to the para-
> lytic, "Son, your sins are forgiven you." And some
> of the scribes were sitting there and reasoning
> in their hearts, "Why does this Man speak blas-
> phemies like this? Who can forgive sins but God
> alone?" But immediately, when Jesus perceived in
> His spirit that they reasoned thus within them-
> selves, He said to them, "Why do you reason about
> these things in your hearts? Which is easier, to say
> to the paralytic, 'Your sins are forgiven you,' or to
> say, 'Arise, take up your bed and walk'? But that
> you may know that the Son of Man has power on
> earth to forgive sins"—He said to the paralytic, "I
> say to you, arise, take up your bed, and go to your
> house."
>
> —MARK 2:5–11

The paralytic was healed by Jesus because of the faith
of his friends. Jesus responded to "their faith." Likewise
believers can pray for others.

10. Medicine

God has built the human body to respond to attacks by
defense systems. God has placed within the body healing
processes. The Bible uses interchangeably the words *lamas*
and *therapuo*. So, God may use medicine to heal, aiding
the natural defenses of the body.

Recently I had knee-replacement surgery. I was

surprised to be rebuked by many brothers and sisters in Christ for having this operation rather than relying solely on prayer and intercession for my healing. I was disturbed by this until my friend Charles Carrin reminded me that it was Jesus Himself who said, "Those who are well have no need of a physician, but those who are sick."

God uses a myriad of approaches to effect healing for His children, and most people can be healed unless it is time for them to go home.

CHAPTER SIXTEEN
Healing Through Communion

THE LORD'S SUPPER or Communion has been taken too lightly by the church. For that reason negative physical affects, including sickness, weakness, and death, have come upon many.

> What! Do you not have houses to eat and drink in? Or do you despise the church of God and shame those who have nothing? What shall I say to you? Shall I praise you in this? I do not praise you. For I received from the Lord that which I also delivered to you: that the Lord Jesus on the same night in which He was betrayed took bread; and when He had given thanks, He broke it and said, "Take, eat; this is My body which is broken for you; do this in remembrance of Me." In the same manner He also took the cup after supper, saying, "This cup is the new covenant in My blood. This do, as often as you drink it, in remembrance of Me." For as often as you eat this bread and drink this cup, you proclaim the Lord's death till He comes.
>
> —1 CORINTHIANS 11:22–26

The Blood Covenant

Notice that the Lord's Supper is a "covenant" meal. In fact, it is symbolic of a "blood oath or covenant." The word *covenant* in the Old Testament is *berith*. It means "to cut." When covenants were made in the east, animals were killed, their bodies halved, and the covenanting parties would walk between the carcasses on bloody ground; both mingle with the common blood of the animal. Blood represents life, and by pledging upon the blood, they agreed that their lives were joined in the sacred promise and the breaking of the covenant was to forfeit one's life.

In other rituals friends would become blood brothers by cutting their hand or forearm, commingling their blood to ratify the covenant of friendship. By mingling blood, the ritual said that the lives of the two were now one! They had exchanged life for life. These covenants were usually binding for generations.

The New Covenant

In the Lord's Supper Jesus portrays the brutalizing of His body and the shedding of His blood for those who would be in covenant with Him! Communion is the feast whereby we symbolically take in the blood and body of Jesus. His life becomes my life and my life becomes His life!

Jesus called this "the New Covenant." In Greek there are two words for *new*: *neos*, which means new in time—God had promised it before the world was! Yet at the Last Supper, Jesus used the word *kainos*, which speaks of a newness in quality. This covenant was as old as the bloody skins clothing Adam and Eve, as old as the lamb slain by Abel, as old as the wine and bread offering to Abraham by Melchizedek, as old as the offering of Isaac, as old as the temple sacrifices, the day of atonement, the Passover.... Yet it was new in that the shadow became substance, the ritual became reality, and the benefits released were supernatural.

The Symbols of Covenant

The two elements of communion were bread representing His body and wine representing His blood.

The blood—the wine

Now the wine relates to our sins and their forgiveness. Also the wine pictures our victory over the devil. It pictures the life of Jesus taken into the life of the believer.

> But if we walk in the light as He is in the light, we have fellowship with one another, and the blood of Jesus Christ His Son cleanses us from all sin.
>
> —I JOHN 1:7

The body—the bread

The body of Jesus represented by the bread has to do with the health of our bodies.

> But He was wounded for our transgressions, He was bruised for our iniquities; the chastisement for our peace was upon Him, and by His stripes we are healed.
>
>   —ISAIAH 53:5

> Who Himself bore our sins in His own body on the tree, that we, having died to sins, might live for righteousness—by whose stripes you were healed.
>
>   —1 PETER 2:24

Think with me a few moments about the beating of Jesus with the Roman cat-o'-nine-tails. It was vicious, brutal, and often fatal. He received thirty-nine blows, what the Romans believed to be one blow away from death. Many died under this awful beating.

Each of the nine leather thongs contained bits of stone, glass, and metal. In the course of 39 blows the victim would receive 351 stripes. These stripes are for our healing! Strangely enough Passover bread is both striped and pierced!

Jesus was beaten to shreds for our healing! He became unrecognizable for our healing.

> Just as many were astonished at you, so His visage was marred more than any man, and His form more than the sons of men.
>
>   —ISAIAH 52:14

Jesus's body broke the death grip of the Law as well! Now let us return to 1 Corinthians 11:29–30.

> For he who eats and drinks in an unworthy manner eats and drinks judgment to himself, not discerning the Lord's body. For this reason many are weak and sick among you, and many sleep.

Note the word *unworthy*. It is not in the Greek text! Literally it could be translated, "He that eats and drinks, making themselves criminally guilty, does so not understanding the difference between the body and blood of Christ."

You need to discriminate between what the blood did for you and what Jesus's *body* did for you. It was His *body* that released healing! The bread of Communion represents His body. When rightly understood and taken there is healing released by Communion!

The Sad Results of Failure

Church people are weak, sickly, and dying because of a lack of understanding about the Lord's Supper.

1. Weak means infirmity.

2. Sick means illness.

3. Sleep means death.

When you take in the bread of Communion you are taking in His life. The blood ratifies what the bread releases in the covenant with God. By *faith* take the meal that heals!

CHAPTER SEVENTEEN

Six Dimensions of Healing

Having said all of this, it is important to note the exact meaning of Psalm 107:20, "He sent His word and healed them, and delivered them from their destructions."

Sent means to "send away" or "to let loose." *Word* in this verse is the Hebrew *dabar*, which means "spoken word." God's Word must be uttered and unfettered if it is to be the conveyance of healing power!

Jay Snell points out the gathering of healing words in Acts 3 and 4. This is like a cluster of ripe grapes! Each one speaks of an aspect of healing.

1. To be strengthened

> And he took him by the right hand and lifted him up, and immediately his feet and ankle bones received strength.
>
> —Acts 3:7

The word *strength* is *stereoō*. Our word *steroid* comes from that word. Athletes have taken steroids to give them strength. Cortisone is a steroid! God heals by giving you some spiritual steroids!

2. To be healed

> Now as the lame man who was healed held on to Peter and John, all the people ran together to them in the porch which is called Solomon's, greatly amazed.
> —ACTS 3:11

The word *healed* in this verse is the Greek word *iaomai.* This word is used for physical healing twenty-eight times in the New Testament. It means, literally, "to make whole."

3. To be whole

> And His name, through faith in His name, has made this man strong, whom you see and know. Yes, the faith which comes through Him has given him this perfect soundness in the presence of you all.
> —ACTS 3:16

The Greek word here is *holoklēria.* It literally means "whole inheritance." Turn to 1 Thessalonians 5:23:

> Now may the God of peace Himself sanctify you completely; and may your whole spirit, soul, and body be preserved blameless at the coming of our Lord Jesus Christ.

The same root word is used in the above passage. Your inheritance includes a "whole body."

4. To be saved

> If we this day are judged for a good deed done to a helpless man, by what means he has been made well…
>
> —Acts 4:9

"Well" in this verse is the Greek word *sōzō*, which is "salvation." Yes, healing is a part of your salvation!

5. To be cleansed

> Let it be known to you all, and to all the people of Israel, that by the name of Jesus Christ of Nazareth, whom you crucified, whom God raised from the dead, by Him this man stands here before you whole.
>
> —Acts 4:10

"Whole" in this verse comes from the Greek word *hygiēs*, which comes from *hagia* or *holy*. Our word *hygiene* comes from that word. This has to do with cleaning up infections, but consider the implication of the connection of health and holiness.

6. To be given therapy

> And seeing the man who had been healed standing with them, they could say nothing against it.
>
> —Acts 4:14

Here the word *healed* is *therapeuō*. He was given "instant" therapy so that his muscles were strengthened. Some may be healed and have to go to therapy. He was able to leap and jump immediately.

This lame man was healed in six dimensions:

1. He was pumped up with Holy Ghost steroids.

2. He was supernaturally healed.

3. He received his "inheritance of wholeness."

4. He was saved from sickness.

5. He was cleansed.

6. He was given therapy.

Hallelujah! It all was released by the Word of God. The Word answers:

+ Weakness

+ Hopelessness

+ Infection

+ Recovery

CHAPTER EIGHTEEN
Healing in the Last Days

AMERICA'S LEADING EXPENDITURE is health care. Health care benefits make up 30 percent of our gross wages in America!

Healing and health go hand in hand. If one experiences healing, then that person can experience health. Health is the lifestyle of one who is experiencing daily the power of the blood of Jesus Christ. Yet today, despite all our efforts, we face incurable diseases: cancer, HIV, and plagues such as Ebola and avian flu.

Incurable Disease and the Last Days

The Bible warns us of pestilence, plagues, and incurable diseases as we move toward the End Times. Jeremiah the prophet speaks of these latter times.

> For thus says the LORD: "Your affliction is incurable, your wound is severe. There is no one to plead your cause, that you may be bound up; you have no healing medicines. All your lovers have forgotten you; they do not seek you; for I have wounded you with the wound of an enemy, with

the chastisement of a cruel one, for the multitude of your iniquities, because your sins have increased.

"Why do you cry about your affliction? Your sorrow is incurable. Because of the multitude of your iniquities, because your sins have increased, I have done these things to you."

—JEREMIAH 30:12–15

Look at these words:

+ Incurable
+ Severe
+ No medicines
+ Incurable sorrow

Why? These things have come upon us all because of the iniquity of a wicked society. God says through Jeremiah that:

Because of the multitude of your iniquities, because your sins have increased, I have done these things to you.

The word *iniquity* means to take good things and twist them into bad things. Our twisted society and world, the things man has done since the fall of Adam, have brought us to such a day.

> The fierce anger of the LORD will not return until He has done it, and until He has performed the intents of His heart. In these latter days you will consider it.
>
> —JEREMIAH 30:24

This verse declares that "in the latter days you will consider it"! So now we look around us, and all of us are coping with incurable diseases.

Hope for Healing in the Last Days

As covenant believers who have been redeemed from the curse of sin and death, we can find hope in these last days that God will put "none of the diseases on you" (Exod. 15:26). We can have real hope by giving our battles with terminal or incurable illnesses over to God.

> Therefore all those who devour you shall be devoured; and all your adversaries, every one of them, shall go into captivity; those who plunder you shall become plunder, and all who prey upon you I will make a prey.
>
> —JEREMIAH 30:16

Make no mistake; we are involved in a spiritual battle, and our health issues are related to our spiritual condition. This is why it is important that we have an increase of faith in God's power to save, deliver, and heal us.

Forgiving Our Enemies: A Key to Miraculous Healing in the Last Days

Unforgiveness is an often overlooked roadblock to being healed from recurring or even serious illness. The medical community has documented the harmful effects unforgiveness can have on our physical body and how it can prevent healing. Unforgiveness gives way to many dangerous emotions such as bitterness, resentment, and anger. The Bible says that when we confess our sins (unforgiveness is a sin—God says that He will not forgive us if we don't forgive others [Matt. 6:15; 5:23–24, 44–45; 6:9–15; 18:21–35; Mark 11:25; Luke 6:35–38]), we will be healed (James 5:16). We work against the process of healing when we hold onto hurts or offenses.

A story from Ronald Reagan's life illustrates how forgiving the one who hurt you can lead to miraculous healing. After the 1982 attempt on Reagan's life, his response made a lasting impression on his daughter, Patti Davis:

> The following day, my father said he knew his physical healing was directly dependent upon his ability to forgive John Hinckley. By showing me that forgiveness is the key to everything, including physical health and healing, he gave me an example of Christlike thinking.[1]

Tapping Into God's Supernatural Healing in the Last Days

Heidi and Rolland Baker focus their ministry in Mozambique. They serve among a Muslim population that has suffered through droughts, war, and disease for generations. The Bakers are power brokers who know the power of the cross condemns them to victory and to walk in the confidence of the Lord. They have seen blind eyes opened, the deaf suddenly hear, and the dead raised to life as routine events in their ministry and through the ministry of pastors they train throughout the world.

They too have discovered that the secret to releasing the power of God is to dwell in the presence of God through prayer and fasting. They have spent countless hours soaking in the love of God and interceding for those to whom they minister. Their intimacy with God provokes confidence to stand in God's presence and see Him as big as He is. They live in a place rife with external evidence of demonic control—war, disease, famine, and corruption. Yet their internal dwelling is a place of *refuge, a fortress, a secret place of worship and communion*. From that place they embark on their mission to magnify the Lord in the world of men.

The Price of Power

If the power of the cross condemns us to victory, as Graham Cooke says, then we must become believers who have a passionate desire to win. No matter where individuals carry the presence and power of God, they all have one thing in common: the firsthand knowledge that there is a price to pay for the anointing to heal the sick, raise the dead, and perform miracles. A passionate desire to win will overcome the temptation to succumb to discouragement and temper the heartache involved with sharing in the suffering of Christ that comes with becoming a power broker in the kingdom of God. A passionate love for Jesus and knowledge of His passionate love also sustain those who are paying the price of power.

According to Randy Clark:

> If you are to prepare for an increase in power, you must understand that walking in the power of the Holy Spirit involves suffering and a continual humbling process. Not everyone you pray for will be healed. Your heart will ache over those who are desperate for a touch from God and don't receive the miracle they seek.
>
> One night I watched John Wimber pray for people gathered together in a Methodist church. Miraculously, almost everybody was healed when he prayed for them. The power of God was definitely present to heal. The next night, however, no one was healed.
>
> I talked to John about it after the abysmal meeting ended and said, "I don't understand it."
>
> He replied, "You don't get it, do you? I don't have any more sin in my life than I did last night. I don't have any less faith tonight than I did last

night. Last night I came here, put my fat hand out and said, 'Come, Holy Spirit.' I just blessed what I saw God do. Last night when everyone got healed I didn't go to bed thinking I'd done anything great or I was some great man of God. And tonight I'm not going to be feeling like I am a great failure either. It wasn't me either time. And tomorrow I'm going to get up and do it again."[2]

Draw Near to God

In these last days it is necessary to walk in the kind of confidence and humility that John Wimber exemplified. We must know that we are God's people and He is our God, so that when we go out to pray for people to be healed—or even when we are standing in faith for our own healing—we can be sure that it is God who does the work. All we can do is draw near to Him, expecting that He will keep His Word.

> "Their nobles shall be from among them, and their governor shall come from their midst; then I will cause him to draw near, and he shall approach Me; for who is this who pledged his heart to approach Me?" says the Lord. "You shall be My people, and I will be your God."
>
> —Jeremiah 30:21–22

Here are four secrets to attaining or maintaining biblical health even in these last days. These secrets will also empower you to pray for others who need to receive the blessing of biblical health.

1. Have a passionate faith

> Trust in the LORD with all your heart, and lean not on your own understanding.
>
> —PROVERBS 3:5

This may seem like an oversimplification, but we are not called to trust in God just a little bit. Back in chapter 3 we talked about giving God our ears; the idea here is the same. We must give God our complete trust.

2. Have a purposeful walk

> In all your ways acknowledge Him, and He shall direct your paths.
>
> —PROVERBS 3:6

Once you give your complete trust to God, you must know that He will guide your way. But God's guidance is not enough; He will show you where to walk, but you must choose to walk!

3. Have a godly life

> Do not be wise in your own eyes; fear the LORD and depart from evil.
>
> —PROVERBS 3:7

Part of the Christian's walk is to consciously leave behind the sins of the past. This idea is, in a way, the reverse of the teaching of Psalm 1:1. There we see that there is a progression of walking in ungodly counsel, which leads to standing in the path of sinners, which culminates in sitting with scoffers. Departing from evil is simply following the path that God has illumined for you.

4. Have a generous life

> Honor the LORD with your possessions, and with the firstfruits of all your increase; so your barns will be filled with plenty, and your vats will overflow with new wine.
>
> —PROVERBS 3:9–10

As a servant of Christ, you are an ambassador in a foreign land. Most ambassadors and foreign diplomats are known, especially in the movies, for taking advantage of diplomatic immunity, a policy whereby diplomats are given safe passage, are not susceptible to lawsuit or prosecution under the host country's laws, and are not required to surrender any item that is considered the property of their home nation. As ambassadors for Christ, we do not have to surrender our healthy inheritance for what the world is suffering with. We are protected and given safe passage from all disease and illness. We are not held by the same laws as those who are not part of God's kingdom, and in Him, we can take full advantage of our kingdom diplomat immunity! This is God's desire for us.

Behold, I will bring it health and healing; I will heal them and reveal to them the abundance of peace and truth. And I will cause the captives of Judah and the captives of Israel to return, and will rebuild those places as at the first. I will cleanse them from all their iniquity by which they have sinned against Me, and I will pardon all their iniquities by which they have sinned and by which they have transgressed against Me. Then it shall be to Me a name of joy, a praise, and an honor before all nations of the earth, who shall hear all the good that I do to them; they shall fear and tremble for all the goodness and all the prosperity that I provide for it.

Thus says the LORD: "Again there shall be heard in this place—of which you say, 'It is desolate, without man and without beast'—in the cities of Judah, in the streets of Jerusalem that are desolate, without man and without inhabitant and without beast."

—JEREMIAH 33:6–10

Notice what God promises in these verses:

- ✦ Healing
- ✦ Revelation
- ✦ Deliverance
- ✦ Cleansing
- ✦ Prosperity

The end result is health, strength, and long life.

> It will be health to your flesh, and strength to your bones.
>
> —PROVERBS 3:8

> For by me your days will be multiplied, and years of life will be added to you.
>
> —PROVERBS 9:11

Some Facts About Healing

Many would, I think, be surprised to learn that the Bible does not regard healing as a miracle unless it is considered incurable.

> …to another faith by the same Spirit, to another gifts of healings by the same Spirit, to another the working of miracles, to another prophecy, to another discerning of spirits, to another different kinds of tongues, to another the interpretation of tongues.
>
> —1 CORINTHIANS 12:9–10

Also, the Bible does not distinguish between healing through medicine and ministry.

> In that region there was an estate of the leading citizen of the island, whose name was Publius, who received us and entertained us courteously for three days. And it happened that the father of

> Publius lay sick of a fever and dysentery. Paul went
> in to him and prayed, and he laid his hands on him
> and healed him. So when this was done, the rest
> of those on the island who had diseases also came
> and were healed.
>
> —ACTS 28:7–9

In this account, both Paul and Luke, the physician, were present and both healed. The Greek word for "were healed" is the word *therapeuō* (the root of our word "therapy") and indicates that both medicinal and miraculous healing took place there in Malta.

It is also a hard truth that sickness is not always healed, and even if it is, it may not be on our timetable. Consider what Paul wrote to Timothy:

> Erastus stayed in Corinth, and I left Trophimus
> sick in Miletus.
>
> —2 TIMOTHY 4:20, NIV

The fact is, sickness and difficulty may be for God's glory.

> Now a man named Lazarus was sick. He was from
> Bethany, the village of Mary and her sister Martha.
> This Mary, whose brother Lazarus now lay sick, was
> the same one who poured perfume on the Lord and
> wiped his feet with her hair. So the sisters sent word
> to Jesus, "Lord, the one you love is sick."
>
> When he heard this, Jesus said, "This sickness
> will not end in death. No, it is for God's glory so

that God's Son may be glorified through it." Jesus loved Martha and her sister and Lazarus. Yet when he heard that Lazarus was sick, he stayed where he was two more days.

—JOHN 11:1–6, NIV

In conclusion, it is very important to understand four points about health and healing.

1. Health is a lifestyle.
2. Incurable issues require a dimensional breakthrough—eternity must interrupt time.
3. Health issues and gifts of health are tied to the church. The gifts operate for those connected to the body—the church.
4. Miracles are tied to the glory of God. The glory of God rests in the church.

The fall of Adam has allowed Satan to rob the earth of its health, to poison its atmosphere, and unleash deadly plagues! But Jesus Christ redeemed to us all those things that were stolen, including biblical health.

Now to Him who is able to do exceedingly abundantly above all that we ask or think, according to the power that works in us, to Him be glory in the church by Christ Jesus to all generations, forever and ever. Amen.

—EPHESIANS 3:20–21

CHAPTER NINETEEN
Do You Want to Be Healed?

I N JOHN 5:6, Jesus asked a physically challenged man who had been waiting to be healed for over three decades this question: "'Do you want to be made well?'"

Before concluding, let's take a closer look at this man and his situation.

I Have No Man

For a span of thirty-eight years he had known nothing but sickness and infirmity. His one hope was the provision made by God at the pool of Bethesda. (Bethesda, or *Beth Hesda*, meaning the "house of mercy," was a spring of water that was known for the miracles there wrought by God.) He lay there every day waiting for the waters to be miraculously stirred by the visitation of an angel, for when the waters were troubled, the first to enter the water would be healed of their infirmity.

He lay there among the multitude of sick, blind, lame, and paralyzed with the hope that today might be the day of his miraculous deliverance and healing. His paralysis, however, made the possibility of reaching the waters before others in the crowd virtually impossible.

For thirty-eight years this man had a lifestyle of being sick, waiting for an angel to stir the waters. Jesus confronted the man with this blunt, almost insulting question! Jesus then released healing for the man and he walked.

I must conclude this book with the same question. Do you want to be healed? If so, are you willing to do whatever Jesus may require? What if you must change churches? Will that destroy your sense of tradition or comfort? What if you must be anointed by spit and mud? Would you be willing to look foolish in the eyes of men? What if you must expose your weakness? Would your pride prove itself to be god to you? What if you must cry aloud and beg? What if you must hang out with weird people who have faith?

You must understand that as you lie, helplessly bound in infirmity, by the pool *you have a man to help you*! His name is Jesus!

When you look at the verses of Scripture, the key to healing is the presence of Jesus. You must believe the Word, live in Jesus's presence, connect with a true faith community, and embrace all of God's gifts. Your healing will come.

> Hear the footsteps of Jesus,
> He is now passing by,
> Bearing balm for the wounded,

Healing all who apply;
As He spake to the suff'rer
Who lay at the pool,
He is saying this moment,
"Wilt thou be made whole?"[1]

NOTES

CHAPTER 1
HEALING AND THE ABUNDANT LIFE

1. *The Robe*, directed by Henry Koster, (1953; Los Angeles: Twentieth Century Fox Home Entertainment, 2001), DVD.

2. "Healing at the Fountain" by Fanny Crosby. Public domain.

CHAPTER 2
HEALING AND THE MYSTERY OF ILLNESS

1. Rev. James R. Boyd, *The Westminster Shorter Catechism With Analysis, Scriptural Proofs, Explanatory and Practical Influences, and Illustrative Anecdotes* (Philadelphia: Presbyterian Board of Education, 1857).

2. "Jesus, Keep Me Near the Cross" by Franny Crosby. Public domain.

CHAPTER 4
JESUS THE HEALER

1. Benjamin Breckinridge Warfield, *Counterfeit Miracles*. Public domain.

Chapter 5
Jesus Healed by the Word

1. "The Word of God Shall Stand" by Frank C. Huston. Public domain.

CHAPTER 10
JESUS HEALED THROUGH DELIVERANCE

1. James Marler, "A Demonic Encounter: The Day I Knew Demons Were Real," *Reflections on the Spirit* (Cleveland, TN: Alicorn Publishing, 2002).

CHAPTER 18
HEALING IN THE LAST DAYS

1. Patti Davis, "To Illustrate Forgiveness: Angels Don't Die," *Leadership Magazine*, 1997, 70.

2. As quoted by Randy Clark in *Shifting Shadows of Supernatural Power* (Shippensburg, PA: Destiny Image Publishers, 2006).

CHAPTER 19
DO YOU WANT TO BE HEALED?

1. "Wilt Thou Be Made Whole?" by William J. Kirkpatrick. Public domain.

Fundamental Truths for the Spirit-Filled Believer

Find clear biblical answers about how the Holy Spirit can work in your life with The Foundation on the Holy Spirit series by Pastor Ron Phillips.

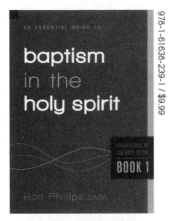

978-1-61638-239-1 / $9.99

978-1-61638-240-7 / $9.99

978-1-61638-492-0 / $9.99

978-1-61638-493-7 / $9.99

10464